Smoothies for Cyclists

Optimal Nutrition Guide and Recipes to Support the Cycling Athlete's Training (Food for Fitness Series)

Lars Andersen

Published by Nordic Standard Publishing

Atlanta, Georgia USA

ISBN 978-1-484145-09-8

Lars Andersen

What Our Readers Are Saying

"Tasty and helps with my training? I thought I must be dreaming!"

★★★★☆ **Terry D. Harris (Vincent, IA)**

"I started to see results much faster than I expected I would"

★★★★☆ **Stanford N. Cecil (Waco, TX)**

"Very informative and easy to follow"

★★★★☆ **Jo J. Pogue (Princeton, ME)**

Exclusive Bonus Download: Fitness & Exercise

This book covers everything there is to know about fitness & exercise. In fact, some people have called it the " The Fitness Professor " !

It's like having your very own fitness & exercise instructor that you can refer and ask questions anytime that you need to!

In this ebook, you'll discover the essential tips to stay away from bad illnesses, how to stay fit & be in a healthy life style:

- Knowing about fitness, health and exercise
- Carbohydrates diet as your fitness & exercise plan
- Fitness for muscles and exercise for building mass
- How to reduce fats and cholesterol that are affecting our health
- Using green tea as the best remedy in diet to improve your health status
- The basic of aerobics cross training
- And much more...

This ebook is overflowing with awesome information and great fitness & exercise tips!

You deserve to have a well shaped body, strong and free of illness that you could ever dream of.

<u>Go to the end of this book for the download link for this Bonus!</u>

Thank you for downloading my book. Please REVIEW this book on Amazon. I need your feedback to make the next edition better. Thank you so much!

Books by Lars Andersen

<u>The Smoothies for Runners Book</u>

<u>Juices for Runners</u>

<u>Smoothies for Cyclists</u>

<u>Juices for Cyclists</u>

<u>Paleo Diet for Cyclists</u>

<u>Smoothies for Triathletes</u>

<u>Juices for Triathletes</u>

<u>Paleo Diet for Triathletes</u>

<u>Smoothies for Strength</u>

<u>Juices for Strength</u>

Paleo Diet for Strength

Paleo Diet Smoothies for Strength

Smoothies for Golfers

Juices for Golfers

Table of Contents

Disclaimer

Smoothies for Cyclists

"It's not about the bike" - Lance Armstrong

Endurance cyclists performing at top level in long distance events such as the Tour de France consume around 7000 calories per day. That's a huge caloric intake when you consider that the daily requirement for an average male is around 2550 calories. The difference between the two highlights the extreme importance of fuelling your body appropriately for the specific demands that will be placed upon it.

If you regularly take part in cycle races of any distance, your average energy expenditure is around 9-12 calories per minute, depending on your body weight. However, as a leisure cyclist, your average energy expenditure is around 5-8 calories per minute. This means that if you are a cycling enthusiast, regularly cycling two or three times per week for an hour or two at a time, consuming 7000 calories per day would *not* lead to improvements in your cycling performance but would in fact have a detrimental effect on your performance - and overall enjoyment - as a result of becoming an overweight cyclist!

At every level of involvement, it's not just the quantity of calories consumed that matters but also the quality of those calories. An elite Tour de France cyclist could gain 1300 calories from a typical fast-food meal of a burger, fries and a shake but five such meals a day could in no way be considered adequate nourishment for the demands of the event. In order to energize your body and fuel your performance, your daily diet must contain the correct balance of nutrients. Smoothies provide a deliciously convenient way to boost your consumption of quality calories and to get that essential balance. This not only improves your overall health, it also helps to increase your pedal power.

Daily Energy Requirements

The foods you eat on a daily basis are your body's only source of energy so getting the right mix of nutrients to fuel your body can be likened to getting the right mix of fuel to power your car. A balanced diet contains a healthy mix of carbohydrates, protein, fats, vitamins and minerals, and calculating your daily energy requirements can be summarized as follows:

Sedentary lifestyle – your body weight in pounds x 14 = your estimated daily caloric requirement.

For example, a non-active individual weighing 150 pounds requires 2100 calories daily.

Moderately active lifestyle – your body weight in pounds x 17 = your estimated daily caloric requirement.

For example, a leisure cyclist weighing 150 pounds and cycling for one or two hours each week at an easy to moderate intensity requires 2550 calories daily.

Active lifestyle – your body weight in pounds x 20 = your estimated daily caloric requirement.

For example, a keen cyclist weighing 150 pounds, cycling four or five times each week for more than two hours each time at a moderate to high intensity, and perhaps taking part in a race every other weekend, requires 3000 calories daily.

The more physically active you are on a daily basis, the more calories you need to fuel the increase in activity.

Energy Sources for Cyclists

Carbohydrates

Carbohydrates provide the main source of energy for cyclists. These can be split into two categories:

Simple carbohydrates - found in sugary foodstuffs such as candy, cakes and soft drinks; also in glucose found in honey, fruit and vegetables; fructose, also found in fruit and honey; lactose, found in milk and dairy products; maltose, found in sprouting grains, malted wheat and barley, and malt extract; and in sucrose, found in table sugar, fruit and vegetables, and foods or drinks with added sugar. Other sources of sugar are molasses, dextrose, corn syrup and invert syrup.

Complex carbohydrates - found in starchy foods such as bread, pasta, and potatoes. These carbohydrates are described as "the athlete's best friend" as they provide the main source of fuel for working muscles.

Complex carbohydrates are broken down for use by the body more slowly than simple carbohydrates, thereby providing a slower release of energy, but all carbohydrates are converted into glucose and glycogen before they can be used to fuel everyday activities and exercise. While cycling, the working muscles are fuelled by glucose in the blood, and by glycogen from stores in the liver and in the muscles. Glucose and glycogen are inter-convertible. When the body has a sufficient supply of glucose, carbohydrates are converted to glycogen and stored, but if glucose is in short supply, glycogen is converted to glucose ready for use. The process of digesting carbohydrates helps to maintain a balance between the levels of glucose in the blood and the levels of glycogen stored in the liver and muscles.

One gram of carbohydrate provides four calories. However, your body can only store a limited amount of glycogen, with the muscles able to store enough for up to around two hours of intense exercise. After exercising, your body's ability to store glycogen is elevated. This period of around 30 minutes is known as the "glycogen window" and consuming appropriate foods in this window helps replenish glycogen stores, promote muscle repair and restoration, and thereby aid recovery after a long or intense cycle ride.

Fat

Fats also provide energy with one gram of fat providing nine calories. They act as a carrier for fat-soluble vitamins, including vitamins A, D, K, and E, they provide insulation for your body, and they protect vital organs. Contrary to popular belief, we needfat in our diet, but we don't need it in the quantities we tend to consume in the average Western diet!

The average Western individual has around 60 times more energy stored in their body as fat than energy stored as glycogen in the liver and muscles. During endurance sports such as long-distance cycling, the body conserves as much of its glycogen reserves as possible by using some of its fat stores for energy. However, compared to carbohydrate, fat is a very slow source of energy, meaning that as the intensity of the exercise increases, the body switches to using glycogen to provide a faster release of energy. The bonus of fat consumption for cyclists is that it provides over twice the calories of carbohydrate, weight for weight, without creating too much bulk in the stomach.

Protein

Protein is essentially the body's muscle-builder but it is only used as a source of energy if your body's glycogen stores have been depleted. However, protein is of particular value to endurance athletes, such as long-distance cyclists, as it plays an important role in repairing the muscles that may suffer damage through repetitive wear and tear.

Benefits of Smoothies for Cyclists

Smoothies provide a convenient method of consuming the quality calories required to fuel cycling activities without the need to eat bulky meals that may lead to an uncomfortable ride. A pre-ride smoothie provides the carbohydrates needed for energy and also the fluids needed for essential hydration without overloading the stomach. A post-ride smoothie helps to replenish your body's glycogen stores and to promote muscle repair after an intense effort. This not only helps to boost your energy levels for the rest of the day, it also helps to ensure that your glycogen stores are topped up ready for the next ride.

Pre-Ride Smoothie

Base ingredients for a typical pre-ride smoothie might include:

Berries

Fresh or frozen berries provide carbohydrates for energy, but they also contain:

Antioxidants - these vitamins and minerals help to protect against free radicals, potentially harmful chemicals produced by the body as part of its defense against bacteria. Strawberries offer a rich source of vitamin C, providing a boost the immune system and helping to maintain the health of the respiratory tract.

Potassium - essential for healthy muscle and nerve function.

The moderately slow release of energy provided by the fructose found in fruit helps to keep you going on a longer ride.

Cooked Oatmeal

Adding oatmeal provides a further source of carbohydrate and a slow release of energy. It is also relatively high in protein, helping to promote muscle growth and repair.

Honey

Honey provides energy boosting simple carbohydrates in the form of glucose and fructose.

Water or Ice Cubes

Adding water or ice changes the consistency of the smoothie, so the exact amount required is a matter of personal choice. More liquid means more hydration but it can also mean greater potential for sloshing around in your stomach. A process of trial and error is needed to discover the consistency that works best for you.

There are no hard and fast rules when it comes to choosing pre-ride smoothie ingredients and alternative or **additional sources of carbohydrate** include:

Bananas

Ripe bananas are easily digested and also provide a good source of potassium.

Fruit Juice

Fruit juice can add flavor to a smoothie along with vitamin C and additional liquid, allowing you to alter the consistency to your taste without diluting the carbohydrate value. Any added juices should always be 100 percent fruit juice.

Maple Syrup or Agave Syrup

Syrup can be used in addition to honey to add to the carbohydrate content or in place of honey to provide a different flavor. Maple syrup contains zinc and manganese, both known to help boost the immune system, and agave syrup provides a slower release of energy than honey and fruit, making it a useful energy source for endurance cyclists. Another benefit of agave is its anti-inflammatory properties.

Cooked Rice

Cooked rice provides additional carbohydrate and protein, with the added benefit of providing a slow release of energy to help keep you pedaling for longer.

Alternative or **additional sources of protein** include:

Milk

Milk provides high quality protein, calcium, zinc and phosphorus, essential for a healthy immune system and strong bones.

Non-fat Yogurt

Yogurt also boosts the calcium and phosphorus content of a smoothie, helping to give a creamy texture without adding bulk.

A smoothie containing fruit, honey, oats and dairy consumed around 60 to 90 minutes before a ride is an effective combination, providing a moderately fast-acting source of energy which is accelerated by the blending process. Leisure cyclists or cyclists with the goal of weight loss will find that a smoothie containing only the base ingredients will satisfy their needs, but if cycling with the goal of improving your performance, additional carbohydrates will be required. As a general rule, you should add 0.45 grams of carbohydrate per each pound of body weight before a moderate intensity ride of two to four hours, and 0.68 grams of carbohydrates per pound of body weight before an intense ride of four or more hours.

As an example, 50 gram carbohydrate add-ons include:

Two tablespoons of honey

One small pot of yogurt

Two large bananas

One large mango

Three or four apples

Three or four pears

One glass of pure orange juice

175 grams of cooked brown rice

Post-Ride Smoothie

A smoothie consumed within the 30 minute post-ride glycogen window is an effective way to help your body recover from your ride and also replenish depleted glycogen stores so that you'll be fully energized for your next ride. During this window, the enzymes in your body responsible for making glycogen are more active, meaning that glycogen stores can be replenished faster by consuming carbohydrate-rich foods. However, it's not unusual to find that you are not at all hungry immediately after a ride and a full meal is not something you can stomach. A post-ride "recovery" smoothie provides a readily digestible alternative. Adding a small amount of protein to create a 3:1 ratio of carbohydrates to protein provides an ideal recovery combination. Protein stimulates the action of insulin which boosts glycogen replacement by aiding the transportation of glucose from the blood to the muscles.

The ideal ingredient combination in a post-ride smoothie might include:

Fruit

Any fruit combination will provide carbohydrates so it comes down to personal taste. Fruits with antioxidant properties can help to reduce the effects of any muscular damage. Vitamin C, vitamin E, and beta-carotene are particularly effective at limiting the potentially damaging effects of free radicals. Popular choices include:

Strawberries

Raspberries

Papaya

Banana

Mango

Kiwi fruit

Fruits with orange or dark yellow flesh provide a good source of beta-carotene, and fruits with red flesh offer a good source of lycopene. Beta-carotene is the plant form of vitamin A, and the combination of beta-carotene and lycopene is thought to be very effective in terms of protecting your body against free radicals.

Honey

Honey provides instantly useable carbohydrates and adds sweetness to a smoothie.

Milk or Yogurt

Milk provides whey protein and casein protein. Whey is a fast acting protein which helps to reduce the effects of muscle damage immediately after an intense ride, and casein is a slow acting protein which helps to continue the repair process long after the ride. **Whey powder** provides a convenient alternative source of protein.

Flax Seeds

Flax seeds, also known as linseeds, are high in omega-3 essential fatty acids which are known to be beneficial in reducing inflammation. They also contain B vitamins, magnesium and manganese. B vitamins are involved in the release of energy from food, magnesium plays an important role in muscle contraction, and manganese is a vital component of many enzymes involved in energy production.

Peanut Butter

Peanuts are high in healthy unsaturated fat, making them high in energy giving calories. They also contain B vitamins, phosphorus, iron, copper and potassium. Iron is essential in the production of hemoglobin, the pigment in red blood cells which carries oxygen in the blood, and it is also needed to manufacture myoglobin, a pigment which stores oxygen in the muscles. Copper helps to protect against free radical damage and plays an important role in helping the body to absorb iron from food. Peanuts are also a good source of vitamin E but an alternative source could also be **almond butter**. The antioxidant properties of nuts give your immune system a boost and the mineral content may also help to relieve leg cramps, a common complaint among endurance cyclists. Leg cramps are the result of fatigue and an electrolyte imbalance. Adding peanut or almond butter to a smoothie helps to restore the balance.

Electrolytes are particles that circulate in your blood and help to regulate your body's fluid balance. Restoring the electrolyte balance is important after every ride but the longer or more intense the ride, the more stress your body will suffer. Endurance rides can lead to muscle soreness and inflammation but a post-ride smoothie can help to minimize the damage and speed the recovery process.

Fluids and Hydration

Adequate hydration is essential at all times and of particular importance to long-distance cyclists. Fluids must be carried on a ride and small sips taken frequently. According to his book, *The Lance Armstrong Performance Program*, elite distance cyclists aim to drink three to four ounces of fluid every 10 minutes. This can be in the form of plain water or a drink specially formulated for sport containing a ratio of four grams of carbohydrate to one gram of protein.

Remaining hydrated during a ride is essential as fluid in your blood transports glucose to the working muscles and takes away the metabolic by-products. Hydration levels can be boosted before a ride by drinking a large glass of water and replaced after a ride in the same way, but adding water or ice to a pre or post-ride smoothie provides a practical way to take in essential fluids without overloading your stomach.

Water in Fruits

The water content of the fruits included in your smoothie can significantly increase the overall fluid content.

Melon - 94 percent water

Grapefruit - 91 percent water

Strawberries - 89 percent water

Oranges - 86 percent water

Peaches - 86 percent water

Apples - 84 percent water

Grapes - 79 percent water

Bananas - 71 percent water

Green Smoothies for Cyclists

A green smoothie is essentially a smoothie made by combining green leafy vegetables with fruit. The resulting green color can be off-putting but a green smoothie is an effective way for cyclists to get the nutrition they need both pre and post-ride.

For example, adding watercress to a pre-ride smoothie boosts the fluid content as it contains 91 percent water, and also provides an additional source of vitamin C, beta-carotene and iron. Other dark green salad leaves such as spinach and arugula are also rich sources of vitamin C and beta-carotene, and can add new and interesting flavors to a smoothie. However, in many cases, adding green leaves to a fruit smoothie does not alter the fruity taste, making it a great way for non-vegetable lovers to get their greens!

A mix of 60 percent fruit and 40 percent green leafy vegetables works best, and popular green smoothie combinations include:

Spinach with bananas, strawberries and peach - the sweetness of the fruit overrides the flavor of the spinach, providing an antioxidant-rich smoothie.

Kale with oranges and kiwi fruit - kale contains iron, calcium, vitamin C and beta-carotene, with citrus fruits also providing a rich source of vitamin c and antioxidants.

Collard greens with banana, apple, pear and dates - collard greens contain omega-3 fatty acids, thereby providing anti-inflammatory properties, and dates are good source of iron and calcium.

Adding fresh herbs to a green smoothie can also boost the nutritional benefits as well as the flavor. Popular choices include:

Parsley - one cup of parsley contains 2 grams of protein. It is also rich in calcium and provides iron, copper, magnesium, potassium, zinc, phosphorus, beta-carotene and vitamin C.

Dill – adds a sweet flavor to a smoothie and contains calcium, iron, manganese, vitamin C, and beta-carotene.

Sorrel - provides iron, magnesium and calcium.

Basil - provides beta-carotene, iron, potassium, copper, manganese and magnesium

Coriander - provides a mild, peppery flavor along with anti-inflammatory properties, vitamin C, iron and magnesium.

Choosing Smoothie Ingredients

There are virtually no limits in terms of choosing smoothie ingredients other than in your imagination. Experimentation is the only way to discover the flavor combinations that work best for you. The fresher your ingredients, the more nutritional value they hold, but it is worth noting that frozen produce can represent a good choice when fresh foods may have spent a little longer than ideal on the grocery store shelf. Organic produce will generally offer a healthier choice, but non-organic produce still provides the nutrients you need to fuel your body during cycling activities and boost your overall health.

Foods with a relatively low glycemic index provide a slower release of energy and therefore represent good choices for a pre-long-distance ride smoothie. Foods with a higher glycemic index provide a more instant energy boost, making them good choices for post-ride smoothies when your glycogen stores are depleted. Almost all fruits and vegetables have a low glycemic index but apples, oranges and pears, for example, offer a slower energy release than bananas, grapes and cherries. The sugar contained in a fruit smoothie is absorbed more slowly than the sugar in a fruit juice because of the fiber content. Adding green leafy vegetables or herbs increases the fiber content and therefore slows the absorption process further, helping to avoid a sugar spike and subsequent crash.

Smoothie Tips

Use fresh ingredients whenever possible. Frozen versions may provide better quality and a wider choice when seasonal fruits are in limited supply. Canned fruits are often in sugary syrup so choose versions that contain only fruit juice.

Use pure fruit juice rather than juice made from concentrate to ensure the maximum nutrient value.

Use low-fat or fat free milk or yogurt to add protein without adding fat.

Adding peanut butter or almond butter provides a healthy source of unsaturated fat.

Bananas provide a creamy texture but alternatives include mango, papaya, peach, coconut and avocado.

A smoothie will keep in the refrigerator for up to 24 hours so a post-ride recovery smoothie can be prepared ahead of time, making it even easier to take advantage of the glycogen window.

Using tried-and-tested smoothie recipes is a great way to get started as they take all of the guess work out of finding the best balance of nutrients and combinations of flavors. However, you will soon discover the combinations that please your taste-buds the most and the boost in your energy levels will ensure that you continue to try new and different flavors … and you will be creating your very own adventurous recipes before you know it.

General Information about Your Smoothies

These smoothies are divided into 3 categories, each designed to meet the nutritional needs of cyclist in three moments:

Pre-ride smoothies - for rides lasting 2 to 4 hours;

Pre-ride smoothies - for rides lasting 4 or more hours;

Post-ride smoothies.

The great majority of the ingredients in these recipes has a low Glycemic Index.

When the recipes call for fruit juice, always choose one that is made of pure fruit.

If you can't find the fresh fruit you need for a recipe, feel free to replace it with frozen. Frozen fruits have the same nutritional content as the corresponding fresh fruits.

You can adjust the consistency of your smoothie adding some ice cubes to the recipe before blending and/or straining before serving.

Pre-Ride Smoothies - for Rides Lasting 2 to 4 Hours

These smoothies were developed to provide an adequate amount of Carbohydrates to a 150 pounds person. You can adjust the amount of carbohydrates by adding one of the following by each extra 5 pounds of your body weight:

2 tsps. of oatmeal;

½ tsp. of honey;

1 tbsp. of flax seed;

2 tsp. of high fiber cereal;

¼ tbsp. of fruit jam;

1 tsp. of seeded raisins;

½ tbsp. of dried apricots;

3 ½ tbsps. of reduced fat milk;

2 ½ tbsps. of low fat yogurt.

1. Simple Banana Smoothie

Preparation time	5 minutes
Ready time	5 minutes
Serves	1
Serving quantity/unit	290 G / 10 Ounces
Calories	345 Cal
Total Fat	3 g
Cholesterol	2 mg
Sodium	98 mg
Total Carbohydrates	67 g
Dietary fibers	8g
Sugars	28 g
Protein	15g

Prepare your smoothie combining the following ingredients in a food processor:

- ½ cup of oats
- ¾ cup of sliced banana
- ½ cup of fat free yogurt
- 2 ice cubes
- 1 tsp. of honey

2. Orange and Strawberry Smoothie

Preparation time	5 minutes
Ready time	5 minutes
Serves	1
Serving quantity/unit	390 G /14 Ounces
Calories	295 Cal
Total Fat	2 g
Cholesterol	6 mg
Sodium	86 mg
Total Carbohydrates	68 g
Dietary fibers	5g
Sugars	57 g
Protein	6g

Prepare your smoothie combining the following ingredients in a food processor:

- 1 tbsp. of honey
- ½ cup of high fiber cereal
- ¾ cup of strawberries
- ½ cup of fat free strawberry yogurt
- ½ cup of orange juice

3. Apple Pie Smoothie

Preparation time	5 minutes
Ready time	5 minutes
Serves	1
Serving quantity/unit	290 G /10 Ounces
Calories	314 Cal
Total Fat	3 g
Cholesterol	0 mg
Sodium	14 mg
Total Carbohydrates	70 g
Dietary fibers	8 g
Sugars	37 g
Protein	6g

Prepare your smoothie combining the following ingredients in a food processor:

- ¾ cup of sliced apple
- ½ cup of oats
- 1 tsp. of cinnamon
- 1 tsp. of lemon zest
- 1 tsp. of lemon juice
- ¾ tbsp. of honey

4. Vanilla and Raisins Smoothie

Preparation time	5 minutes
Ready time	5 minutes
Serves	1
Serving quantity/unit	200 G / 7 Ounces
Calories	305 Cal
Total Fat	2 g
Cholesterol	7 mg
Sodium	94 mg
Total Carbohydrates	67 g
Dietary fibers	3 g
Sugars	52 g
Protein	9g

Prepare your smoothie combining the following ingredients in a food processor:

- ½ cup of seedless raisins
- 1 tsp. of lemon juice
- ½ cup of fat free vanilla yogurt

5. Raspberry and Coconut Smoothie

Preparation time	5 minutes
Ready time	5 minutes
Serves	1
Serving quantity/unit	390 G / 14 Ounces
Calories	383 Cal
Total Fat	14 g
Cholesterol	0 mg
Sodium	38 mg
Total Carbohydrates	66 g
Dietary fibers	10g
Sugars	35 g
Protein	2 g

Prepare your smoothie combining the following ingredients in a food processor:

- 1 tbsp. of agave syrup
- ½ cup of shredded coconut meat (fresh)
- ¾ cup of raspberries
- 1 cup of pure raspberry juice

6. Chocolate and Almonds Smoothie

Preparation time	5 minutes
Ready time	5 minutes
Serves	1
Serving quantity/unit	400 G /14 Ounces
Calories	448 Cal
Total Fat	17 g
Cholesterol	20 mg
Sodium	103 mg
Total Carbohydrates	67 g
Dietary fibers	6 g
Sugars	51 g
Protein	12g

Prepare your smoothie combining the following ingredients in a food processor:

- 1 cup of reduced fat milk
- 2 tbsps. of almonds
- 1 ½ tbsps. of semi-sweet chocolate pieces
- ¾ cup of sliced frozen banana
- 1 tbsp. of maple syrup

7. Yellow Smoothie

Preparation time	5 minutes
Ready time	5 minutes
Serves	1
Serving quantity/unit	300 G /11 Ounces
Calories	311 Cal
Total Fat	1 g
Cholesterol	5 mg
Sodium	66 mg
Total Carbohydrates	68 g
Dietary fibers	3g
Sugars	62 g
Protein	6g

Prepare your smoothie combining the following ingredients in a food processor:

- 1 tbsp. of honey
- ¼ cup of lemon zest sorbet
- ½ cup of fat free pineapple yogurt
- ½ cup of sliced peach
- ¼ cup of diced pineapple
- 1 tsp. of cinnamon

8. Hidden Carrots Smoothie

Preparation time	5 minutes
Ready time	5 minutes
Serves	1
Serving quantity/unit	400 G / 14 Ounces
Calories	284 Cal
Total Fat	1 g
Cholesterol	0 mg
Sodium	43 mg
Total Carbohydrates	71 g
Dietary fibers	4g
Sugars	62 g
Protein	3 g

Prepare your smoothie combining the following ingredients in a food processor:

- ½ cup of chopped carrot
- ½ cup of sliced mango
- 1 cup of pure orange juice
- 1 ½ tbsps. of honey

9. Apple and Pear Green Smoothie

Preparation time	5 minutes
Ready time	5 minutes
Serves	1
Serving quantity/unit	450 G /16 Ounces
Calories	263 Cal
Total Fat	1 g
Cholesterol	0 mg
Sodium	33 mg
Total Carbohydrates	67 g
Dietary fibers	5 g
Sugars	58 g
Protein	2g

Prepare your smoothie combining the following ingredients in a food processor:

- ½ cup of apple
- ½ cup of pear
- 1 cup of spinach
- 1 cup of apple juice
- 1 tbsp. of honey

This is another great option to add more greens to your diet. Spinach is a very rich vegetable constituting an excellent source of Vitamin K and a very good source of other vitamins such as A, C and folate and minerals such as manganese, potassium, magnesium and iron.

Pre-Ride Smoothies - for Rides Lasting 4 or More Hours

Like the pre-ride smoothies for a 2 to 4 hours ride, these smoothies were also designed to provide an adequate amount of Carbohydrates to a 150 pounds person. Nothing to worry about if you weigh less than 150 pounds, but if you weight more than this, consider adjusting the amount of carbohydrates by adding one of the following by each extra 5 pounds of your body weight.

1 tbsp. of oatmeal;

¾ tsp. of honey;

1 ½ tbsps. of flax seed;

1 tbsp. of high fiber cereal;

1 tsp. of fruit jam;

1 ½ tsps. of seeded raisins;

1 tbsp. of dried apricots;

5 tbsps. of reduced fat milk;

3 tbsps. of low fat yogurt.

10. Greek Smoothie

Preparation time	5 minutes
Ready time	5 minutes
Serves	1
Serving quantity/unit	350 G / 12 Ounces
Calories	544 Cal
Total Fat	9 g
Cholesterol	10 mg
Sodium	131 mg
Total Carbohydrates	102 g
Dietary fibers	4g
Sugars	86 g
Protein	24 g

Prepare your smoothie combining the following ingredients in a food processor:

- 2 tbsps. of honey
- 1 7oz. container of Greek yogurt
- ½ cup of raisins
- 1 tbsp. of nuts

11. Tropical Smoothie

Preparation time	5 minutes
Ready time	5 minutes
Serves	1
Serving quantity/unit	350 G / 12 Ounces
Calories	502 Cal
Total Fat	6 g
Cholesterol	6 mg
Sodium	73 mg
Total Carbohydrates	103 g
Dietary fibers	9g
Sugars	57 g
Protein	14g

Prepare your smoothie combining the following ingredients in a food processor:

- 1 ½ tsps. of honey
- ¾ cup of papaya sliced
- ¼ cup of strawberries
- ¾ cup of oats
- ½ cup of fat free strawberry yogurt

12. Two Berries Smoothie

Preparation time	5 minutes
Ready time	5 minutes
Serves	1
Serving quantity/unit	300 G / 11 Ounces
Calories	438 Cal
Total Fat	3 g
Cholesterol	10 mg
Sodium	242 mg
Total Carbohydrates	102 g
Dietary fibers	7g
Sugars	72 g
Protein	8g

Prepare your smoothie combining the following ingredients in a food processor:

- ½ cup of blueberries
- ¼ cup of dried cherries
- 1 cup of cereal with red fruits
- ½ tbsp. of honey
- ½ cup of reduced fat milk

13. Winter Flavors Smoothie

Preparation time	5 minutes
Ready time	5 minutes
Serves	1
Serving quantity/unit	350 G / 12 Ounces
Calories	549 Cal
Total Fat	9 g
Cholesterol	7 mg
Sodium	112 mg
Total Carbohydrates	103 g
Dietary fibers	10 g
Sugars	23 g
Protein	17g

Prepare your smoothie combining the following ingredients in a food processor:

- ¾ cup of banana
- ½ cup of fat free vanilla yogurt
- ¾ cup of oats
- 1 tsp. of unsweetened cocoa powder
- 1 ½ tbsps. of. agave syrup

14. Raspberry Sorbet Smoothie

Preparation time	5 minutes
Ready time	5 minutes
Serves	1
Serving quantity/unit	400 G / 14 Ounces
Calories	438 Cal
Total Fat	1 g
Cholesterol	0 mg
Sodium	1 mg
Total Carbohydrates	104 g
Dietary fibers	8 g
Sugars	50 g
Protein	5g

Prepare your smoothie combining the following ingredients in a food processor:

- ½ cup of raspberry sorbet
- 1 cup of frozen berries
- ¾ cup of cooked brown rice
- ½ tbsp. of brown sugar
- 1 tbsp. of raspberry jam

15. Peanut Butter &Friends Smoothie

Preparation time	5 minutes
Ready time	5 minutes
Serves	1
Serving quantity/unit	300 G / 11 Ounces
Calories	594 Cal
Total Fat	15 g
Cholesterol	10 mg
Sodium	139 mg
Total Carbohydrates	105 g
Dietary fibers	11g
Sugars	54 g
Protein	118g

Prepare your smoothie combining the following ingredients in a food processor:

- 1 tbsp. of peanut butter
- 1 tbsp. of Grape Fruit Jam
- ½ cup of grapes
- ¼ cup of dates
- ½ cup of milk
- ¾ cup of oatmeal

16. Pear and Kiwi Smoothie with Kale

Preparation time	5 minutes
Ready time	5 minutes
Serves	1
Serving quantity/unit	550 G / 19 Ounces
Calories	417 Cal
Total Fat	1 g
Cholesterol	0 mg
Sodium	42 mg
Total Carbohydrates	104 g
Dietary fibers	5g
Sugars	76 g
Protein	4 g

Prepare your smoothie combining the following ingredients in a food processor:

- ¾ cup of kiwi
- ½ cup of pear
- 1 cup of kale
- ½ cup of 100% pear juice
- 1 ½ tbsps. of honey
- ½ cup of cooked brown rice

17. Dried mango and Pineapple Smoothie

Preparation time	5 minutes
Ready time	5 minutes
Serves	1
Serving quantity/unit	200 G / 7 Ounces
Calories	423 Cal
Total Fat	0 g
Cholesterol	0 mg
Sodium	65 mg
Total Carbohydrates	107 g
Dietary fibers	5g
Sugars	72 g
Protein	0 g

Prepare your smoothie combining the following ingredients in a food processor:

- 8 slices of dried mango (around 90g)
- ½ cup of diced pineapple
- 1 tbsp. of agave syrup

18. Watermelon and Guava Smoothie

Preparation time	5 minutes
Ready time	5 minutes
Serves	1
Serving quantity/unit	350 G / 12 Ounces
Calories	465 Cal
Total Fat	2 g
Cholesterol	5 mg
Sodium	78 mg
Total Carbohydrates	106 g
Dietary fibers	9g
Sugars	92 g
Protein	9g

Prepare your smoothie combining the following ingredients in a food processor:

- ½ cup of seedless watermelon
- ½ cup of golden raisins
- ½ cup of your favorite fat free fruit yogurt
- ½ cup of guava
- ½ tbsp. of brown sugar

Post-Ride Smoothies

These smoothies constitute great combinations of carbohydrates and protein sources which will be essential to give your body the right nutrients enhancing its recovery after your ride. Also in these recipes, if you weight more than 150 pounds, it is better to adjust the nutritional content of your smoothie by adding, for each extra 5 pounds of body weight, one of these:

1 tbsp. of oatmeal;

1 tbsp. of almonds;

1 tbsp. of nuts mixture;

1 tbsp. of peanuts;

1 tbsp. of flaxseeds;

1 tbsp. of sesame seeds;

2 tbsps. of milk;

2 tbsps. of yogurt.

19. Banana, Apple and Peanut Butter Smoothie

Preparation time	5 minutes
Ready time	5 minutes
Serves	1
Serving quantity/unit	450 G / 16 Ounces
Calories	599 Cal
Total Fat	20 g
Cholesterol	15 mg
Sodium	320 mg
Total Carbohydrates	79 g
Dietary fibers	8 g
Sugars	64 g
Protein	24 g

Prepare your smoothie combining the following ingredients in a food processor:

- 2 tbsps. of peanut butter
- 1 cup of fat free vanilla yogurt
- ½ cup of sliced banana
- ½ cup of sliced apple
- ½ cup of dried apples
- 1 tsp. of honey

20. Kiwi Strawberry Smoothie

Preparation time	5 minutes
Ready time	5 minutes
Serves	1
Serving quantity/unit	500 G / 18 Ounces
Calories	583 Cal
Total Fat	10 g
Cholesterol	10 mg
Sodium	184 mg
Total Carbohydrates	101 g
Dietary fibers	15g
Sugars	77 g
Protein	29g

Prepare your smoothie combining the following ingredients in a food processor:

- ¾ cup of tofu
- ½ cup of strawberry yogurt
- ¼ cup of strawberries
- ¼ cup of dried cherries
- ½ cup of kiwi
- 2 tbsps. of powdered milk
- 1 tbsp. of honey

21. Fig Honey and Nuts Smoothie

Preparation time	5 minutes
Ready time	5 minutes
Serves	1
Serving quantity/unit	450 G / 16 Ounces
Calories	586 Cal
Total Fat	20 g
Cholesterol	63 mg
Sodium	316 mg
Total Carbohydrates	77 g
Dietary fibers	5g
Sugars	50 g
Protein	26g

Prepare your smoothie combining the following ingredients in a food processor:

- ¾ cup of part skim ricotta
- ¼ cup of reduced fat milk
- 2tbsps. of honey
- 3 medium fresh figs
- 1 tbsp. of nuts

22. Fruit and Granola Smoothie

Preparation time	5 minutes
Ready time	5 minutes
Serves	1
Serving quantity/unit	400 G / 14 Ounces
Calories	573 Cal
Total Fat	19 g
Cholesterol	20 mg
Sodium	254 mg
Total Carbohydrates	78 g
Dietary fibers	8g
Sugars	50 g
Protein	26g

Prepare your smoothie combining the following ingredients in a food processor:

- 5 tbsps. of instant skim milk powder
- ½ cup of cubed melon
- ½ cup of sliced banana
- ½ cup of granola
- ¾ cup of milk

23. Tasty Beet Smoothie

Preparation time	5 minutes
Ready time	5 minutes
Serves	1
Serving quantity/unit	500 G / 18 Ounces
Calories	488 Cal
Total Fat	4 g
Cholesterol	0 mg
Sodium	137 mg
Total Carbohydrates	98 g
Dietary fibers	16g
Sugars	48 g
Protein	27g

Prepare your smoothie combining the following ingredients in a food processor:

- ½ cup of cubed beet
- ½ cup of sliced carrot
- 1 cup of 100% orange juice
- 1 tbsp. of strawberry jam
- 1 tbsp. of honey
- 5 tbsps. of nutritional yeast

Beets are a great source of fiber, folate, vitamin C, potassium and manganese.

24. Peach and Chocolate Smoothie

Preparation time	5 minutes
Ready time	5 minutes
Serves	1
Serving quantity/unit	500 G / 18 Ounces
Calories	560 Cal
Total Fat	15 g
Cholesterol	70 mg
Sodium	233 mg
Total Carbohydrates	77 g
Dietary fibers	5g
Sugars	65 g
Protein	31g

Prepare your smoothie combining the following ingredients in a food processor:

- 1 cup of milk
- 1 scoop (around 30g) whey powder
- 1 cup of sliced peach
- 2 tbsps. of peach jam
- 2 tbsps. of semi-sweet chocolate pieces

25. Fresh Lemon and Papaya Smoothie

Preparation time	5 minutes
Ready time	5 minutes
Serves	1
Serving quantity/unit	500 G / 18 Ounces
Calories	577 Cal
Total Fat	20 g
Cholesterol	77 mg
Sodium	314 mg
Total Carbohydrates	72 g
Dietary fibers	2g
Sugars	53 g
Protein	29g

Prepare your smoothie combining the following ingredients in a food processor:

- ½ cup of lemon zest sorbet
- ¾ cup of sliced papaya
- 1 tbsp. of honey
- 1 cup of part skim ricotta

26. Blueberries and Banana Vegetarian Smoothie

Preparation time	5 minutes
Ready time	5 minutes
Serves	1
Serving quantity/unit	550 G / 19 Ounces
Calories	469 Cal
Total Fat	10 g
Cholesterol	0 mg
Sodium	38 mg
Total Carbohydrates	81 g
Dietary fibers	14g
Sugars	40 g
Protein	28g

Prepare your smoothie combining the following ingredients in a food processor:

- ¾ cup of tofu
- 1 cup of blueberries
- 1 cup of sliced banana
- 1 tbsp. of blueberry jam
- 2 tbsps. of nutritional yeast

27. Coconut Pineapple Smoothie

Preparation time	5 minutes
Ready time	5 minutes
Serves	1
Serving quantity/unit	400 G / 14 Ounces
Calories	401 Cal
Total Fat	3 g
Cholesterol	0 mg
Sodium	293 mg
Total Carbohydrates	76 g
Dietary fibers	16g
Sugars	34 g
Protein	25g

Prepare your smoothie combining the following ingredients in a food processor:

- 1 cup of coconut water
- ¼ cup of dried pineapple
- ½ cup of fresh diced pineapple
- 5 tbsps. of nutritional yeast

28. Vegetarian Smoothie with Prunes and Almond butter

Preparation time	5 minutes
Ready time	5 minutes
Serves	1
Serving quantity/unit	500 G / 18 Ounces
Calories	598 Cal
Total Fat	26 g
Cholesterol	0 mg
Sodium	52 mg
Total Carbohydrates	77 g
Dietary fibers	12g
Sugars	42 g
Protein	27g

Prepare your smoothie combining the following ingredients in a food processor:

- 1 6oz. container of mixed berry yogurt
- ¾ cup of tofu
- ¼ cup of prunes
- ½ cup of raspberries
- 1 ½ tbsps. of almond butter

29. Mango and Peach Smoothie with Biscuits

Preparation time	5 minutes
Ready time	5 minutes
Serves	1
Serving quantity/unit	500 G / 18 Ounces
Calories	502 Cal
Total Fat	8 g
Cholesterol	13 mg
Sodium	212 mg
Total Carbohydrates	79 g
Dietary fibers	4g
Sugars	55 g
Protein	28g

Prepare your smoothie combining the following ingredients in a food processor:

- ½ cup of sliced peach
- ¼ cup of mango
- ½ cup of mango sorbet
- 1 cup of Greek yogurt
- 5 whole wheat, plain, rectangular tea biscuits

30. Guava, Strawberry and Oatmeal Smoothie

Preparation time	5 minutes
Ready time	5 minutes
Serves	1
Serving quantity/unit	450 G / 16 Ounces
Calories	552 Cal
Total Fat	10 g
Cholesterol	13 mg
Sodium	88 mg
Total Carbohydrates	83 g
Dietary fibers	11 g
Sugars	37 g
Protein	36g

Prepare your smoothie combining the following ingredients in a food processor:

- ½ cup of guava
- ¼ cup of strawberry
- ¾ cup of oatmeal
- 1tbsp. of honey
- 1 cup of Greek yogurt

31. Peach and Apricots Smoothie with Watercress

Preparation time	5 minutes
Ready time	5 minutes
Serves	1
Serving quantity/unit	400 G / 14 Ounces
Calories	462 Cal
Total Fat	7 g
Cholesterol	0 mg
Sodium	49 mg
Total Carbohydrates	83 g
Dietary fibers	15 g
Sugars	57 g
Protein	29g

Prepare your smoothie combining the following ingredients in a food processor:

- ½ cup of sliced peach
- ½ cup of banana
- ¼ cup of dried apricots
- 1 cup of watercress
- ½ cup of tofu
- 3 tbsps. of nutritional yeast
- 1 tbsp. of honey

32. High Fiber Smoothie

Preparation time	5 minutes
Ready time	5 minutes
Serves	1
Serving quantity/unit	550 G / 19 Ounces
Calories	419 Cal
Total Fat	7 g
Cholesterol	13 mg
Sodium	188 mg
Total Carbohydrates	80 g
Dietary fibers	18g
Sugars	49 g
Protein	29g

Prepare your smoothie combining the following ingredients in a food processor:

- ¾ cup of sliced peach
- ¾ cup of pineapple
- 1 cup of Greek yogurt
- ½ cup of high fiber cereal
- 1 tbsp. of honey

33. Banana, Chocolate and Pecan Nuts Smoothie

Preparation time	5 minutes
Ready time	5 minutes
Serves	1
Serving quantity/unit	300 G /11 Ounces
Calories	521 Cal
Total Fat	14 g
Cholesterol	50 mg
Sodium	192 mg
Total Carbohydrates	73 g
Dietary fibers	8g
Sugars	38 g
Protein	28g

Prepare your smoothie combining the following ingredients in a food processor:

- ½ cup of chocolate sorbet
- 2 tbsps. of pecan nuts
- ¾ cup of banana
- ¼ cup of oatmeal
- 1 scoop (around 30g) of whey powder

34. Cranberries and Cherry Smoothie

Preparation time	5 minutes
Ready time	5 minutes
Serves	1
Serving quantity/unit	550 G / 19 Ounces
Calories	414 Cal
Total Fat	2 g
Cholesterol	47 mg
Sodium	159 mg
Total Carbohydrates	71 g
Dietary fibers	5g
Sugars	48 g
Protein	28g

Prepare your smoothie combining the following ingredients in a food processor:

- 1 cup of cranberries
- 1 cup of Cherry
- 1 cup of fat free cherry yogurt
- 1 scoop (around 30g) of whey powder with strawberry flavor

35. Melon and Papaya Smoothie with Broccoli

Preparation time	5 minutes
Ready time	5 minutes
Serves	1
Serving quantity/unit	550 G / 19 Ounces
Calories	420 Cal
Total Fat	3 g
Cholesterol	50 mg
Sodium	189 mg
Total Carbohydrates	77 g
Dietary fibers	6g
Sugars	60 g
Protein	25g

Prepare your smoothie combining the following ingredients in a food processor:

- ¾ cup of melon
- ¾ cup of papaya
- ½ cup of broccoli
- 1 cup of 100% pineapple juice
- ½ tbsp. of honey
- 1 scoop (around 30 g) of whey powder

Exclusive Bonus Download: Fitness & Exercise

Download your bonus, please visit the download link above from your PC or MAC. To open PDF files, visit http://get.adobe.com/reader/ to download the reader if it's not already installed on your PC or Mac. To open ZIP files, you may need to download WinZip from http://www.winzip.com. This download is for PC or Mac ONLY and might not be downloadable to kindle.

This book covers everything there is to know about fitness & exercise. In fact, some people have called it the " The Fitness Professor " !

It's like having your very own fitness & exercise instructor that you can refer and ask questions anytime that you need to!

In this ebook, you'll discover the essential tips to stay away from bad illnesses, how to stay fit & be in a healthy life style:

- Knowing about fitness, health and exercise
- Carbohydrates diet as your fitness & exercise plan
- Fitness for muscles and exercise for building mass
- How to reduce fats and cholesterol that are affecting our health

- Using green tea as the best remedy in diet to improve your health status
- The basic of aerobics cross training
- And much more...

This ebook is overflowing with awesome information and great fitness & exercise tips!

You deserve to have a well shaped body, strong and free of illness that you could ever dream of.

Visit the URL above to download this guide and start achieving your weight loss and fitness goals NOW

One Last Thing...

Thank you so much for reading my book. I hope you really liked it. As you probably know, many people look at the reviews on Amazon before they decide to purchase a book. If you liked the book, could you please take a minute to leave a review with your feedback? 60 seconds is all I'm asking for, and it would mean the world to me.

******

Books by This Author

The Smoothies for Runners Book

Juices for Runners

Smoothies for Cyclists

Juices for Cyclists

Paleo Diet for Cyclists

Smoothies for Triathletes

Juices for Triathletes

Paleo Diet for Triathletes

About the Author

Lars Andersen is a sports author, nutritional researcher and fitness enthusiast. In his spare time he participates in competitive running, swimming and cycling events and enjoys hiking with his two border collies.

Lars Andersen

Published by Nordic Standard Publishing

Atlanta, Georgia USA

NORDICSTANDARD
PUBLISHING

12796715R00037

Printed in Great Britain
by Amazon.co.uk, Ltd.,
Marston Gate.